Our Friends the Saints

W.H. LITHO COMPANY
Brooklyn, N.Y.

Nihil Obstat, John M. Fearns, S.T.D.
Imprimatur ✠ Francis Cardinal Spellman, Archbishop, New York
Cum permissu superiorum

Saint Agatha—The Pure Virgin

Saint Agatha was very beautiful. People looked at her and said, "Oh, she is the fairest girl alive." But Agatha was also very pure and good. She loved Jesus Christ very much. She promised God she would never marry. "All my love is Yours," she said. "I will live and die for You." Now it happened that the Governor of Sicily where Agatha lived heard of her beauty. So he sent for her. Soldiers came and arrested her. "You are a Christian," they said. "So you must go to jail." "Dear Lord Jesus," she prayed, "I belong to You. Do not let this tyrant have power over me." He made love to her. But she refused him. So he threw her into prison. The governor was sure Agatha would be so afraid of prison that she would consent to love him. Instead, she made the wicked woman who was her jailer love God too. So the Governor ordered her to be tortured. She was not afraid. Then he ordered her to be beaten. "Dear Jesus," she cried, "come and take me." And Jesus came and took her home to heaven. Her feast is February 5th.

St. Aloysius Gonzaga

Aloysius was the son of a very famous and noble family. They expected him to make a name for himself in the world. Instead, he promised God he would never marry. He asked to love God and Our Lady alone. When he was very young, he became a Jesuit. From the very start, he was as holy as he could be. He kept his soul as pure as the whitest snow. He loved Mary with all his heart. He stayed for hours on his knees before Christ in the Blessed Sacrament.

But he was a brave young man. When a terrible sickness came over the city, Aloysius went out to care for the sick. Once he brought home a very sick old man and nursed him in his own bed. He wanted very much to be a priest. But God wanted to show young people that even the very young can be saints. So he took Aloysius early with him to Heaven. He is the special patron of boys and girls and is their model of purity. His Feast is: June 21st.

St. Agnes—Martyr

Agnes was only twelve when the Roman soldiers arrested her. They were killing all Christians in those days. But first they dragged her to the statue of a false goddess. "Offer prayers and incense to Minerva," they ordered her. Instead, brave little Agnes lifted her arms and prayed aloud to Jesus Christ. So they put handcuffs on her. She was so tiny that the cuffs slipped off her wrists.

Then they whipped her cruelly. They said they would stop if she gave up Jesus Christ. Even the pagans wept to see her tortured that way. Next they dragged her through the streets for the people to laugh at. Instead, some of them tried to save her. Then a young man asked her to marry him. "I will save you if you do," he promised. "I belong to my Savior alone," she answered. With one stroke of the sword, the soldiers killed this brave little girl. Her Feast is: January 21st.

Saint Andrew—Apostle

Andrew was just a poor fisherman in Galilee. He had a brother whose name was Simon Peter.

One day he heard a great preacher, John the Baptist. He left his boats and fishing nets, and followed John. And John said, "Someone is coming who is greater than I." So when Jesus came, Andrew left John to follow Jesus. He ran and told Simon Peter. Peter went to Jesus. They both became Apostles.

Andrew was the Apostle who found the little boy with the loaves and fishes. Our dear Lord used these to feed thousands of people. That was a great miracle. Jesus made Andrew one of His first Bishops. "Go, teach everyone the Good News," Jesus said. So after the Ascension of our Lord into heaven, Andrew went to Greece. Some listened and became Christians. But some hated Andrew because they hated Jesus. So they nailed Andrew to a Cross. Andrew sang with joy because, like Jesus, he could die on the Cross. He hung for two days on the Cross telling everyone about Jesus. Then he went gloriously to heaven. His Feast is November 30th.

St. Angela—Friend of Girls

Angela de Merici was a lovely young Italian woman. She knew many poor girls. Most of them did not know about Jesus Christ. Many of them had never heard much about the lovely Mother of God. Many of them were sinful and bad.

So she gathered children around her and taught them about Jesus and Mary. She helped sinful girls to become good once more. She built houses where they could live and be safe from temptation. She found fine, pure, wise young women to teach the children. She wanted sinless girls to help save sinful girls. She took Saint Ursula for her patron. Then she invited good young women and pure, sweet girls to help her. They became the first Ursuline Sisters. They went all over the world teaching and helping little children and girls and young women. Today there are thousands of these Sisters. They all call Saint Angela their Patroness and Holy Mother. Her Feast is: May 31st.

St. Anthony of Padua

When Anthony of Padua died, the children cried in the streets. "Our dear father, Anthony, is dead," they wept. And all the bells of the churches rang of their own accord. Angels came to earth to ring the bells for the death of the saint. Anthony wanted to be a martyr. He wanted to die for the love of Christ. Instead, Our Lord asked him to work among the poor and needy. So Anthony went about Italy working wonderful miracles for the people. He gave them miraculous food. He healed their sicknesses.

Whenever he spoke of Jesus, everyone listened and loved the Savior, too. One night the Divine Child came to visit Anthony. He kissed the saint gently and told him how much He loved him. You have often seen statues of St. Anthony with the Child in his arms. Ever since his death, he has done wonderful things for those who pray to him. He is still the Franciscan Miracle-worker. His Feast is: June 13th.

St. Ann—Mother of Blessed Virgin

Ann was a dear old lady who had been married a long time. But God had never sent her a child. That made her sad. She wanted a baby to brighten her home. She kept praying to God, and God heard her prayer. Her lovely little baby was Mary. But even her happy Mother did not know that this little girl would be the Mother of God.

Ann gave her daughter the best home she could. She sent her to school in the Temple. She loved her very much. All the time, God knew Ann would be the Grandmother of His Son. Because she was so good to Mary, His Mother, Jesus made Ann a great saint. When we pray to her, we know that Jesus, her Grandson, will listen to what she asks for us. Her Feast is: July 26th.

Saint Augustine—Bishop and Doctor of the Church

When Augustine was a young man, he was very clever and bright. His mother, Monica, was a good Catholic. But Augustine couldn't be bothered. He didn't want to believe what Christ taught. He knew that what Christ taught was the truth, but he did not want to be good. He led a very wicked life. All this time, his mother, Monica, wept and prayed. "Make my son a good man," she begged God. "Please make him believe and give up his sins." One day Augustine heard that some of his friends had become Catholics. They were not nearly as bright as he was. "How silly and foolish I am," he thought. "They will go to heaven. But I, to whom God gave such a fine mind, will lose my soul." He ran to his mother and told her he wished to be good henceforth. She was very glad. So he repented of his sins. He studied to be a priest. He became a great Bishop. He did penance for his sins. And he wrote many wonderful books about God and the soul and goodness. He fought untruth and he hated sin. The young man who had been a sinner became the man who was a wise and holy saint. His Feast is August 28th.

St. Barbara—the Brave Martyr

When Barbara was a little girl, her wicked father imprisoned her in a high tower. So Barbara lived in the tower with only the servants who cared for her. And she was very good. One day a priest passed under her tower. He was singing about Jesus Christ. Barbara heard him. She asked him about his song. He told her all about the Savior. Barbara was overjoyed. "I love Jesus too," she cried.

In those days, it was against the law to love Jesus or to be a Christian. So this cruel father dragged his own daughter to the judge. "My daughter is a Christian," he cried. "She is not my daughter any longer." "What shall we do with her?" the judge asked. For he saw that Barbara was good and pure. "Do what the law orders," her father shouted. "Beat her until she is almost dead. Then chop off her head." So the soldiers carried out that cruel order. But suddenly they saw angels coming. The angels carried the soul of Barbara to heaven. Her Feast is: December 4th.

Saint Benedict—Father of Holy Monks

The name Benedict means Blessed. When Benedict was a boy, he realized that he was living in sad, not blessed days. The world was full of savage and evil men. They made war on everybody. They destroyed beautiful buildings and burned wise books. They thought it was amusing to be destructive. They were very cruel. Even the schoolboys were wicked and mean. They laughed at Benedict because he tried to be good. So he ran away from the evil men and the sinful boys. He hid himself in a mountain near Subiaco. He prayed. He studied. He talked with God. He asked God to make cruel men gentle and wicked little boys pure. Soon many people heard about this wonderful young man. They hated war and evil men. So they ran up to the mountain and said to Benedict, "Let us stay with you."

Benedict built beautiful houses which are called monasteries. He dressed the good men as monks. His sister, Saint Scholastica, dressed the women as nuns or sisters. She built convents. In these the men and women prayed. They studied. They loved peace. They asked God to forgive sinners. These men and women were the first Benedictines. His Feast is March 21st.

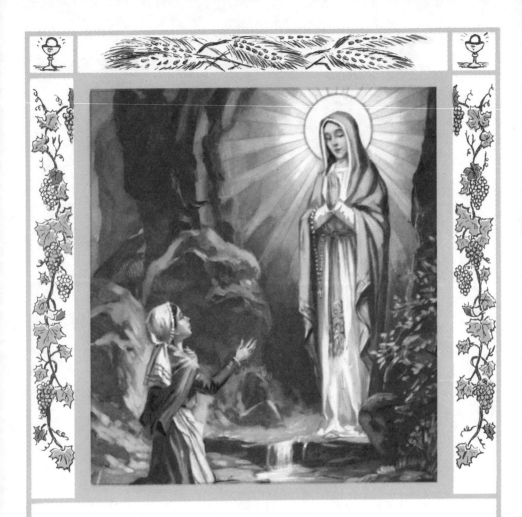

St. Bernadette—of Lourdes

Bernadette's mother and father were very poor. One day Bernadette went to gather firewood. She came to a cave near a flowing river. Her friends played and sang. But Bernadette stood still, her eyes wide with wonder. For she saw a beautiful Lady, who was dressed in blue and white. There were stars around the Lady's head. Roses were on her feet. Bernadette told her parents and friends. At first they did not believe her. But Bernadette saw the lovely Lady again and again. The lovely Lady ordered her to dig a hole at the spot. A fresh, cool spring came bubbling up out of the ground.

Sick people who bathed in it grew well. Many of the blind could see again. "Build here," said the lovely Lady, "a great church. And tell people to pray and do penance and walk in processions." They did all this. Soon the wonderful Shrine of Lourdes was built where miracles happen even to this day. Her Feast is: April 16th.

St. Bernard of Clairvaux

When Bernard went to be a monk and a priest, thirty of his young friends
went with him. Later on, his father became a priest. And all his brothers joined
him in this monastery. He had only one sister. At first she was very gay and
vain. But soon she became a nun, too. That all showed how people loved Bernard
and followed him. He built a great monastery in a valley called Clairvaux. It
was so strict people said, "No one will join." Instead, hundreds came.

The Turks, who hated Christians, were very strong and had great armies.
Bernard taught soldiers how to be fine pure knights. They became the Knights
of the Temple. He led the Christian armies to fight against the Turks. He
carried only a crucifix. But most of all, he loved Christ and Our Lady. As a boy,
as a great priest, even in the army, he wrote beautiful songs to them. Some
of them we sing to this day. His Feast is: August 20th.

St. Brigid—of Ireland

When Brigid was a very little girl, Saint Patrick converted the Irish. She was a very beautiful little girl. Many young men wanted to marry her. "I shall be a nun," she thought. But she never knew she was going to be the first of millions of Irish nuns throughout the world. "Make me ugly," she prayed to God. "Then I can love You alone." God heard her prayer and she became very ugly. With joy she became a sister, a nun. And as soon as she did, God made her more beautiful than ever.

She built a lovely little convent. She tended the cattle herself. Other young women heard about her. They came and asked to join her and be nuns too. Then little girls came to be taught. The sick came to her and asked her to care for them. Often she sold everything she had and gave the money to the poor. So the Irish have called her their patroness ever since. Her Feast is: February 1st.

St. Charles—Borromeo

Charles Borromeo was a rich Italian young man. His family was noble. His uncle was Pope Pius IV. But more than anything, Charles wanted to be a good priest. At that time the Protestant churches had just begun. Besides, because of war and disease, Italy badly needed good priests and fine Catholics.

So Charles became a priest. The Pope made him a Bishop very young. At once he worked hard for the poor. He took care of the sick in their own homes. When he preached, thousands came to hear him. But often he sat by the road and taught one poor man his prayers. He loved the Church because Christ loved it. He brought thousands back to Mass and Holy Communion. He built fine seminaries for priests, and schools for children. In the end, a terrible sickness came to Milan, his city. Charles nursed the sick himself. He laid them on his own bed. He died of the sickness, a martyr of charity. His Feast is: November 4th.

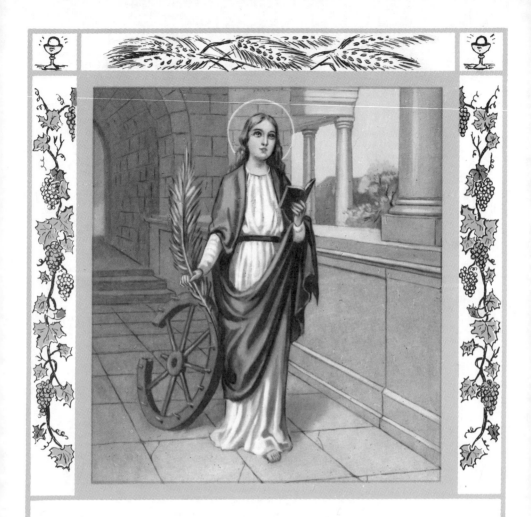

Saint Catherine—of Alexandria

Catherine was a very rich child, being the daughter of noble parents. She was able to go to school and studied very hard. She was always very holy. During her studies she found time to pray quietly to God. In the days of Catherine, the Christians were being persecuted. When Catherine was 18 years old, she went to the Emperor, who was violently persecuting the Christians and told him that he must stop attacking the good poeople and also stop serving false gods. The Emperor was insulted and put her in jail. He said that she must die by being tortured on a spiked wheel.

A miracle happened when she touched the wheel. It fell apart. The Emperor then ordered her head to be cut off. When her head was cut off, the angels from heaven carried her body to Mount Sinai, where later a church and convent was built in her honor. Her Feast is November 25th.

St. Catherine of Sienna—the Dominican

Catherine of Sienna was one of the greatest women that ever lived. When she was a little girl, our dear Lord appeared to her.

"Please give me your heart," He asked.

She gave it willingly. Jesus gave her His Sacred Heart in return.

Many rich men wanted to marry her. Instead, she became a Dominican Sister.

In those days, the Pope did not live in Rome. He had moved to France. Catherine went to see him.

"Holy Father," she said, "your place is in Rome. Come home to your people."

The Pope obeyed this simple little nun.

Many of the princes were furious. They did not want the Pope in Rome. So they tried to elect a false Pope.

Catherine, without fear, told them this was wrong. They listened and obeyed.

The Pope knew she was very wise, and often asked for her advice. She always told him just what Jesus wanted and what would please God.

Although she was only thirty-three when she died, the whole world knew this saintly girl. They loved this brave woman. Her Feast is: April 30th.

St. Christopher—The Christ Bearer

Saint Christopher was a giant and very strong. He was a very brave soldier. "I will serve only the strongest men in the world," he said. So he fought in the army of a great, strong king. But one day the soldier saw the king tremble and grow pale. The king was afraid of Satan. The thought of the Devil frightened him. So Christopher—whose name was then Offero—went to serve the Devil. But soon he found that the Devil was afraid of someone too. Oh, he was very strong, but he was afraid of Jesus. "I will serve Him," said Christopher.

So he went to a river where many travellers came. He carried them across on his strong shoulders. Some day, he thought, Jesus Christ might come that way. Then one day a little Boy came to the river. Christopher hoisted the Boy on his shoulders. He was very light. But as they crossed the river, He got heavier and heavier. "Who are You?" asked the giant. "I am Jesus Christ," said the Boy. "You looked for Me." The giant was very happy. He became a Christian. His Feast is: July 25th.

St. Cecilia—Martyr

Cecilia was a lovely Roman girl. She loved Jesus with all her heart. But a young Roman wanted to marry her. She told him she belonged to Our Lord alone. At first he and his brother were very angry. They tried to force marriage on her. But when the young man walked toward Cecilia, he saw her strong, beautiful Guardian Angel standing at her side.

The young man at once became a Christian. So did his brother. The Roman soldiers came and took all three of them prisoners. They cried, "Offer sacrifice to our gods." But Cecilia, though just a young woman, spoke for all of them. "We love and serve only the true God," she answered. So all three went to Heaven together in martyrdom. Just a few years ago, Cecilia's body was found in its grave in Rome. Though she had been dead for almost eighteen hundred years, her body was still fresh and sweet and beautiful, as if she were asleep. Her Feast is: November 22nd.

Saint Clare—Franciscan

Sometimes we call her St. Clare. Sometimes, St. Clara or St. Claire. Her mother and father were very rich. She lived in a beautiful Italian palace. But she listened to a man named St. Francis of Assisi. He was very like Christ. He loved God. He wanted to be poor. He hoped to save the world from sin. So, when her parents said she could not be a nun, Clare ran away. She cut her hair. She put on old clothes with a rope for her belt. In a little hut, she took her sister, then her mother and some friends. She began the sisters known as the Poor Clares. All day long these sisters pray for sinners. They love God for those who do not love Him. They do penance so that men and women will not lose their souls. Once the army of men who hated Christ came to Assisi. They meant to destroy the city.

St. Clare carried the Blessed Sacrament outside the convent. Only her sisters were around her. But the great army saw her coming. They turned and fled in panic. She had saved the city. Her Feast is August 12th.

Saint Colette—The Franciscan

Colette lived in dangerous times. Three men all pretended to be the real Pope. Many Christians did not know which was the true Pope. But Colette did. When she was a little girl she became a sister. Saint Francis appeared to her in a vision one day. He asked her to love God very much. "And make your sisters good nuns," he begged her. So she did. She showed them how happy a good nun is. She taught them how to take care of the poor and teach little children about Jesus Christ. This little nun loved the Catholic Church very much. So God showed her which was the right Pope. Bravely she told the Bishops and Cardinals what to do. They followed her advice. One Pope was elected and the Church was happy again. The devils hated her because she was so good. They feared her because she loved the Church. So they appeared to her in ugly shapes. They played horrid tricks on her. They tempted her severely. "Stop praying to Jesus," they cried, "and we will stop bothering you." But she only prayed the harder. She died smiling as she was praying to God to forgive all sinners. Her Feast is March 6th.

St. Dominic—Great Preacher

Dominic was a fine, brave young Spaniard. He was a smart student, too. He also loved the poor, and sold even his clothes and books to give money to those who were hungry. In those days, evil men hated Jesus Christ and the truth. They were called Albigenses. They destroyed homes. They burned churches. They killed Catholics, especially priests and nuns. Bravely Dominic decided to gather an army to fight them. Only his was an army of peace. He gathered fine young men and dressed them in white. "I shall call you the Order of Preachers," he said. Nowadays we call these fine priests the Dominicans.

Dominic and his priests went everywhere and taught people the truth about Jesus Christ and goodness. He gathered pure young women and dressed them in white too. "You will pray for sinners," he said. These were the first Dominican nuns. To help him win his battle of peace, Mary, our Blessed Mother, gave him a powerful weapon. It was her Rosary that we pray today. His Feast is: August 4th.

St. Dorothy—Martyr

Dorothy's Mother and Father had both been martyrs. They had bravely died for Jesus Christ. So the soldiers came for the little girl too. They dragged her to the judge. They beat and punished her. But she was faithful to Christ. The judge told two wicked women to take her and show her how silly it was to believe in Our Lord. Instead, she converted them and made them both Christians. The judge was now furious. He ordered the soldiers to treat her more cruelly.

It was mid-winter when she was put to death. There was no fruit and no flowers. A pagan lawyer who hated Christ laughed at her. "Send me some apples or roses from Heaven, will you?" he asked. Just before she died, a little child stood at her side with three apples and three roses. The child was an angel from Heaven. "Take them to the lawyer," Dorothy smiled and died. The lawyer too became a Catholic and died a martyr. Her Feast is: February 6th.

Edward—the Confessor

Edward was one of the greatest Kings of England. He was called the Confessor, because he confessed his belief in Jesus Christ. He admitted proudly that he was a Catholic. He ruled his Kingdom as Christ wanted it ruled. Edward never expected to be king. Indeed, when he was very young, bad men drove him away from England. But the good people remembered him. They knew he would be a fine king. So when he was forty years old, they brought him back. "Be our King!" they cried. And he accepted. He was a very good king.

He was never proud. Instead of sitting on a throne, he walked the streets, talking with people, asking them their troubles, helping them to be happy. He married a very good queen. They lived pure lives. People said, "There is a perfect husband and wife." Often sick people came to him. He touched them and they were cured. All his laws were good. They helped make his people happy. His Feast is: October 13th.

St. Elizabeth—of Hungary

St. Elizabeth, Queen of Hungary, was only twenty-four when she died. But what a beautiful life she had led! Her Father was a king. Her aunt was St. Hedwig. When she was very young, she married Louis, a young nobleman, who soon became king. She was sweet to her husband and loved her children. But she knew that queens should be very good to the poor and the sick. So she took care of them in the palace. She nursed them in the hospitals. Her husband grew angry. "That's no work for a queen," he said.

One day she went to visit the poor. Her cloak was full of provisions. Her husband met her. "Are you carrying food like a servant?" he cried. He pulled open her cloak. Out fell not food but lovely red and white roses. Her husband asked her forgiveness. He knew she was a saint. Her Feast is: November 19th.

St. Francis—of Assisi

Many people say that St. Francis was the man who was most like Our Lord.

He saw how money makes many people bad and proud. So he wanted to be as poor as Our Lord was. He used to say, "I am married to Lady Poverty."

Far in the East are men called Moslems. They do not believe in Jesus Christ. So Francis went to visit them. And though they hated other Christians, they listened to Francis. They thought Jesus must be very fine, because Francis, His friend, was so good.

Once when Francis was praying a wonderful thing happened. God placed in his hands and feet the same marks that Our Lord carried after He was crucified. These are called Stigmata.

Francis preached about Jesus and Mary everywhere.

But so that everyone could hear about Our dear Lord, he gathered men and women to work with him. They worked among the poor people.

They are called the Franciscans. His Feast is: October 3rd.

Saint Frances Xavier Cabrini

From the time she was a very small girl Frances Cabrini wanted to be a missionary. Her home was in Italy. When she grew up she hoped to go all over the world working for God. But there were no Sisters who did the kind of work she thought God wanted her to do. So she began a new order. She named it for the Sacred Heart. Things did not always go well for her. But she knew that the Sacred Heart would take care of her work. She came to America and started hospitals, orphanages and schools in many cities for poor children. She also went to other countries to take care of the poor people there.

She was a small frail lady but she never stopped working. She was doing it to help Jesus save souls and that made her strong.

She is called an American Saint. Her Feast is December 22nd.

St. Frances—of Rome

Frances was a married saint. She had always wanted to be a nun. But her parents wouldn't let her. They insisted she marry a wealthy Roman nobleman. Once she was married, Frances and her husband lived forty years without a hard word or unkind deed. She was a good wife and a saintly mother. Yet she prayed all she could. She took care of the poor, giving them even her own food. But she knew her chief duty was to take care of her house.

Then her troubles came. The enemies of her country captured Rome. They drove her husband away. They threw her son into prison. Frances was very poor. But she accepted all this as God's will. When peace was restored, Frances started a new order of nuns. Then her husband died. And Frances joined the nuns herself. Often she saw her own guardian angel. When she was very good, his light was very bright. If she committed even a fault, his light faded away. Her Feast is: March 9th.

St. George—Martyr

George was a Roman soldier a long time ago. Most people then did not know Our Lord or love Him. But George's parents did. Yet George became a soldier because he was brave and strong. Now the wicked Roman Emperor began to kill the Christians. He ordered his soldiers to arrest and kill them too. George refused to do this. Instead, he told the Emperor that everyone should believe in Jesus Christ and follow him.

The Emperor was furious. He threw the young soldier into prison. He killed him most painfully. And George was happy to be a Martyr for Christ. Soldiers always remember and love young Colonel George. They know he hated and fought evil. So they have always sung songs about him and how he slew the great dragon of sin and evil and cowardice. George is the patron of all brave men. He is the favorite saint of England. His Feast is: April 23rd.

St. Genevieve—Patroness of Paris

Like Saint Joan of Arc, little Genevieve was a shepherdess. She tended her sheep near Paris. One day a great saint passed by. He saw the little girl. "She was very holy," he said. "She will grow holier still." She spent her time in praying, in caring for the sick, in helping the poor. A powerful king attacked Paris. The people were starving. Little Genevieve, quite unafraid, took some of her girl friends, and went out where the enemy could see her. They gathered food and brought it back to the starving Parisians. No one dared to hurt her.

Another time, another general attacked Paris. "Join with me in praying and fasting," she cried to the people. "He will not hurt us or hurt the city." Everyone in Paris did as she said. To their delight, the general and his army packed up and left the city unharmed. Paris loved Saint Genevieve. She is the city's patroness and continues to protect it. Her Feast is: January 3rd.

Saint Gregory the Great—The Pope

Young Gregory's father was very rich. When his father died, Gregory gave all the money he inherited to the poor. Then he went to a monastery and became a monk. He prayed. He studied hard. The Pope of those days heard about this bright young man. He called Gregory to Rome. He made him a Deacon. He sent him on important errands to kings and generals. One day in the market place, Gregory saw some slaves. They told him they were Angles. "You should be Angels," he said. English boys were called Angles in those days. Gregory knew they did not believe in Jesus. You see, he hoped they would be Catholics. When the Pope died, the people made Gregory the Pope. He remembered the English boys. So he sent Saint Augustine to England to tell them about Jesus and to make them Catholics. He sent holy priests to convert the Spanish and the French. Wicked men came rushing into Italy to destroy it. He told them about Jesus, and they became Catholics too. He wrote great books which are still read. He taught people how to sing in Church. We still call these songs the Gregorian Chants. He was one of the greatest Popes that ever lived. His Feast is March 12th.

St. Gertrude—Abbess

Sometimes men and women are so holy that Our Dear Lord comes to talk with them. He likes to bring His Blessed Mother with Him too. And they both tell these saints about Heaven and about the things the Holy Family did on earth. Gertrude was a saint like this. She was a holy nun who lived in a convent of Germany.

She was very clever. When she was a little girl she could write and speak Latin. But most of all, she wanted to know about God. So often Our Dear Lord and His Mother appeared to her. They told her lovely secrets about life after death. They told her how safely we can all reach Heaven. All these things Saint Gertrude wrote down in lovely books. We can still read these books. How sweet it is to be very holy. For then Christ and Mary love to be with us. Her Feast is: November 15th.

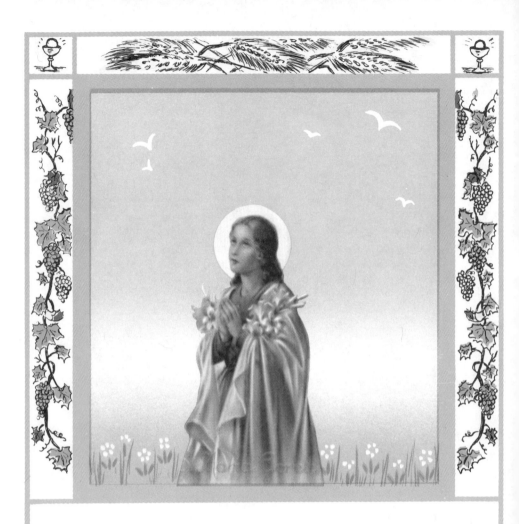

Saint Maria Goretti—Martyr

Not many years ago there lived in Italy a little girl whose name was Marie Goretti. Her mother and father were good but very poor. They lived on a farm in a house with another family. Her father died when Maria was only ten years old. Then her mother had to do the work in the fields. Maria took care of the house and watched over the younger children. One day an older boy of the other family tried to make her commit a sin. But Maria told him that she would rather die than to offend Jesus. The boy got very angry and stabbed her many times with a dagger.

Before she died she told the priest that she forgave the boy who killed her. Jesus said that we must forgive those who harm us. Because she loved Jesus she always did what He said to do. Her Feast is July 6th.

St. Henry—Emperor

When Duke Henry of Bavaria was very young, he had a dream. His patron saint appeared to him and showed him the words, "After six." The young man thought this meant he would die after six years. So he prepared for death. He lived like a saint. Instead, after six years, he was chosen German emperor. But because for six years he had lived like a saint, he was a holy and great emperor.

A wicked man had driven the Pope from Rome. He was sitting on the Pope's own chair. Henry led his army against this bad man, beat him, and brought the Holy Father back to Rome. Whenever he entered the city, his first visit was always to Christ in the Blessed Sacrament. Once Christ rewarded him wonderfully. Henry saw Jesus Himself say Mass in a great church in Rome. Both Henry and his wife, Cunegunda, became great saints. His Feast is: July 15th.

St. Helen—Queen

Helen was a British princess. She became Empress of Rome. At first, she was not a Christian. But she was a good woman. So soon Our Lord gave her the gift of faith. Her strongest son was named Constantine. He was a pagan too. But when he saw his Mother become a Christian, he started thinking.

When Helen was eighty years old, she went to Jerusalem. She wanted to find the Cross on which Our Lord died. She found three crosses buried in Mount Calvary. But when the Cross of Our Lord touched a very sick woman, at once the woman was cured. Later, Helen's son was fighting his strongest enemy. He remembered the Cross his Mother loved. He promised to become a Christian if he won. He did win. And the Cross became the sign of victory for all the world. So St. Helen by her prayers and example made her son, Constantine, the first Christian ruler of the world. Her Feast is: August 18th.

St. Ignatius—a Martyr and a Jesuit

There are two great saints named Ignatius. One was the Bishop of Antioch. Saint John the Apostle taught him to know and love Jesus. The Blessed Sacrament was very dear to his heart. He was always teaching people that Jesus gave them His flesh to eat and His blood to drink. The Roman Emperor was angry because Ignatius would not call him a god. So he dragged him to Rome. "Let the lions devour him!" the Emperor ordered. Ignatius died for the truth.

The other saint who was named Ignatius was a brave soldier and was called Saint Ignatius of Loyola. One day he was wounded badly in battle. When he was getting well, he read the Lives of the Saints. "What they did, I can do!" he thought. And he became the brave soldier of Christ. So he established a new Society of Priests and Brothers. He called it the Society of Jesus. The Feast of Saint Ignatius of Antioch is: February 1st. The Feast of Saint Ignatius of Loyola is July 31st.

Saint Jane—Frances de Chantal

Here is a wonderful saint. She was a saint as a little girl. She was a saint as a wife. When she was a widow, she was a saint. Then she became a nun and was a saint in the convent. When she was a very little girl, Jane Frances asked Our Lady to take care of her. Our Lady always did. Then she married a nobleman. She made him a beautiful home. She loved her husband. She was devoted to her children. But sorrow came to her. Her good husband died. Two children and a sister died. Her friends bothered her to marry again. She was sad and her life was very hard.

At last her children grew up. She knew that God wanted her to be a nun. So with St. Francis de Sales she started the Visitation Order. Her daughters, the Visitation Sisters, to this day pray, do penance, and teach children to love and serve God as Jane Frances did. Her Feast is August 21st.

St. James—the Greater

James was one of the three Apostles Jesus kept nearest to Him. The other two were Peter and John. Like so many of the Apostles, James was a fisherman. He followed Our Lord up the mountain when His face became bright as the sun. He was in the room when Jesus brought the little dead girl back to life. When our dear Lord suffered the Agony in the Garden, James was near Him.

He had a fierce temper which he conquered with difficulty. But he had great faith and preached powerfully. So he was called the Son of Thunder. After Our Lord ascended into Heaven, James bravely went around telling everyone about the Savior. King Herod was angry. He cried, "Do you believe in Jesus Christ?" "Indeed I do," James answered at once. So the soldiers cut off his head with a sword, and he died a martyr. His Feast is: July 25th.

St. Joan of Arc

Joan of Arc did not start out to be a soldier. She was just a simple little shepherd girl. She lived quietly in France with her family. But she loved God very much. And she wanted to see her country free and strong. At that time, her country was fighting the English. The English were winning everywhere. Suddenly Joan heard the voices of angels and saints speaking to her. "Go and save your country," they commanded her.

At first she was afraid. But then she knew God wished it. So she wore armor and rode a horse into battle. The poor French king had not even his crown. The armies were afraid. But Joan led them to victory. She crowned the king in his own palace. Then she said, "My work is done. Let me go back to my sheep." But the king would not let her. Instead, her friends let the enemy capture her. And they burned her to death at the stake. Joan's soul went straight to God. Her Feast is: May 30th.

Saint Jerome—Who Loved the Bible

Saint Jerome was one of the wisest men that ever lived. But at first he was not wise at all. He was just clever. He knew a great deal. And he loved to show off. He liked to have people think him bright. He said things that sounded smart, even if they were not true. But one day Christ spoke to his heart. Then Jerome knew that the truth of Christ was the important truth. He ran away to the desert. He lived in a cave. He prayed. He studied a lot. He read the Gospels over and over again. He became a truly wise man. "Come back to Rome," the Pope said at last. So Jerome obeyed. He knew the Gospels better than anyone in the world. He prepared the Bible so that everyone could read it. But he wanted to return to the land where our Lord had lived. So he left Rome and went to Bethlehem. He wrote beautiful letters to people all over the world. In these letters he told them all about Jesus and His truth. He wrote clear explanations of the Gospels. He prayed to God. And God taught him everything he wanted to know. All this he taught to others. His Feast is September 30th.

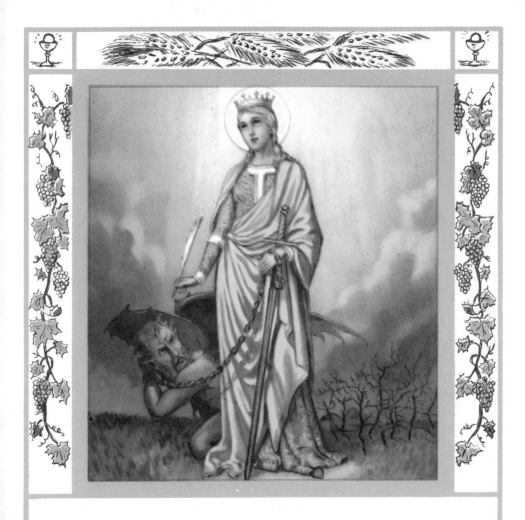

Saint Julia—Virgin Martyr

Julia was a rich noblewoman. She lived in North Africa. The armies that hated Christ captured her country. Julia was seized and sold as a slave. A rich merchant bought her. So this sweet, gentle, well educated woman did the hardest work of his house without pay. But she smiled and was brave. She prayed constantly to Jesus whom she loved. Some time later, her master took her to a pagan place where people were praying to false gods. Julia refused to have part in it. One of the rich Romans was furious. He cried out, "That slave girl is a Christian. She should die." Her owner protected her. But when her owner was asleep, the Roman seized her. "Pray to my gods," he cried. "I will set you free if you do." "Everyone is free," she answered, "If he loves Jesus Christ." So the Roman beat her, nailed her to a cross, and she died a saint and martyr. Her Feast is May 23rd.

St. John—the Beloved Apostle

John was a young fisherman in the Holy Land. One day, our dear Lord said to him. "Come and follow Me." Quickly he left family, boat, everything, and became an Apostle. He saw Our Lord heal the sick and raise the dead. He heard the wonderful things Our Lord taught. He loved Jesus very much. He sat next to Jesus the night when He gave His Apostles their First Communion. Then when the other Apostles ran away from Calvary, John stayed on beside Mary. And Jesus gave this young man Mary for his Mother.

He became a great bishop. He wrote the Fourth Gospel and beautiful letters. He took care of Mary after Jesus ascended into Heaven. The Romans tried to kill him by boiling him in oil. But Jesus protected him. He was not even hurt. Because he was very pure, Jesus loved him best of all the Apostles. His Feast is: December 27th.

St. Joseph

Joseph was a poor carpenter of Nazareth. Yet he came from the royal family of David. And he was pure and good and hard working. God knew He could trust Joseph, so He chose him for a most important task. He became the husband of Mary and the foster father of Our Lord. So he protected Mary on the way to Bethlehem. He was present on the first Christmas. He led Mary and Jesus safely into Egypt when Herod was trying to kill the Child.

Later he worked for them. He made them a sweet little home. He earned money to give them their food and clothing. When Jesus was a big boy, Joseph taught Him the carpenter's trade. Joseph did not live to see Jesus become great and famous. Instead he died happily with Mary at his bedside, and Jesus blessing him. He worked very hard to make life safe and happy for Jesus and Mary. So Jesus has made him the Protector of the Whole Church. His Feast is: March 19th.

Saint Jude—Apostle

Two of Our Lord's relatives were Jude and his brother James. When they were little boys they were playmates of Jesus. And when they grew up they became His Apostles. They were with Him when He changed water into wine at the wedding feast in Cana.

One day a king who had a terrible disease sent for Jesus to come and cure him. But Jesus could not go and He sent Jude. Jude cured the king and told him all about Jesus. The king and most of the people in his kingdom were baptized. Jude and another Apostle, Simon went into many lands telling the people about Jesus and great numbers of them gave up their evil ways and became Christians.

Those who did not want the people to be good hated Jude and had him beaten with clubs and beheaded. His Feast is October 28th.

Saint Stanislaus Kostka—The Boy Saint

Stanislaus Kostka was a young Polish nobleman. His father was a rich man.
So Stanislaus was brought up in the court. Sometimes, men sitting at dinner
said nasty things. When they did, little Stanislaus blushed. It made him ill to
hear men say dirty and unpleasant things. He went away to school with his
big brother. But his big brother was a bully. He treated Stanislaus badly. So
there was nothing to do but run away. He did. His brother followed him with
fast horses. But when they passed Stanislaus on the road, God did not let the
brother see the runaway. On that journey he came to an empty church. Oh,
how he wished he could go to Holy Communion! But there was no priest. How
could he receive? God took care of that. Angels brought Holy Communion to the
boy. He walked all the way from Vienna to Rome. He begged his food. The
Blessed Virgin appeared to him and told him she would take care of him. He
became a Jesuit novice. From the start he showed he was a Saint. He loved to
pray. He was very pure. But Mary, his Mother and ours, came for him on the
Feast of the Assumption and took him to heaven. His Feast is November 13th.

Saint Lawrence—Martyr

Lawrence was a fine young Roman.

He was chosen a deacon. That meant that it was his work to care for the sick and the poor. But the Romans thought he was the treasurer of the Church. So they took him prisoner. "Show us the treasures of the Church," they cried. Lawrence had a great sense of humor. "Gladly," he answered. The Romans hurried after him, expecting to find gold and precious stones. Instead, he led them to the hospital where the poor and the sick lived. "Here are the treasures of the Church," he cried. They were furious. But Lawrence knew how God loves the poor and needy.

In the end, the Romans put him to death. They laid him on a gridiron over a fire. But even there, Lawrence could joke. "Turn me over," he cried, as the fire burned, "for I think I am done on this side." Even in his pain, God gave Lawrence deep happiness.

His Feast is August 10th.

St. Lucy—Martyr

When Lucy was a little girl in Italy, her Mother was very ill. "Let's pray," said Lucy, "and I know you'll get well." So they prayed at the little church of St. Agatha in Rome. Suddenly St. Agatha appeared to Lucy. "Lucy, my sister!" she said to the little girl, "your Mother will be well. But you will die a martyr for Christ." Next morning, her mother was well. Lucy was very rich. In gratitude she gave her money to the poor. Then she became a nun.

It happened that a young man who did not believe in Christ loved Lucy. He wanted her to marry him. When he heard she was a nun, he was furious. He ran to the Roman Judges. "Lucy is a Christian," he said. The soldiers seized her. They threw her into a raging fire. But the flames did not hurt her. God protected her pure body. So the soldiers plunged a sword into her heart. And her pure soul went straight to Heaven. Her Feast is: December 13th.

Saint Leo the Great—The Pope

The name Leo means the Lion. And Saint Leo, the Pope, was a lion in bravery.

The Vandals and Huns, two terrible races, were fighting the Christians of Europe. Besides this, evil men were teaching people lies about Jesus. They were saying what was not true and getting the people confused. Leo became Pope. He had been a smart and wise young man. Now he had to be a brave and very wise Pope. First he went everywhere teaching the truth about our dear Lord. He called together all the wise priests and bishops of the Church. This was the great Council of Chalcedon. They talked and studied and listened. And they went home to teach their people the truth. So people did not believe the evil men any more when they lied about the Savior. But the Vandals and Huns kept coming. They burned cities. They murdered people everywhere. All alone, without weapons, Leo went out to meet them. Their leader Attila was called the Awful Scourge. But when he saw Leo he ordered his armies to cease fighting. Instead of destroying Rome, they turned and went away. The Pope had saved Europe. His Feast is April 11th.

St. Louis—the King of France

Louis was a fine, strong, pure boy. His mother taught him to hate sin. Her name was Blanche. "I love you, my son," she said, "but I would rather see you dead than have you commit one mortal sin." He remembered this all his life. He was made King of France. He determined to be a good and generous king. Each day he found time to hear two Masses. He prayed far into the night.

In those days, the Mohammedans hated Christians. They were trying to destroy the Christian countries. They had great armies. They sailed powerful fleets. It looked as if they would win. But Louis made sure they would not. He gathered a great army and marched out to fight them. He was so brave and fine that the Mohammedans respected him. Some of them asked him to be their king. Yet God did not wish him to win with the sword. He really seemed to lose that war. Only he didn't. The Mohammedans never conquered Christian lands. His Feast is: August 25th.

Saint Luke—The Evangelist

Saint Luke studied medicine when he was a young man and became a great doctor. He was also a skillful painter. One day he heard about Jesus Christ. He knew that Jesus was the Great Physician. He was sure that Jesus was the God who had made all the beautiful world. So Saint Luke followed Jesus as His disciple.

He was very close to Saint Paul and travelled with him. He was a clever writer. So he wrote down all that the Apostles did. This book we call the Acts of the Apostles. Then he went to see Our Lady. He asked her all about the Baby Jesus. He wrote what she told him in the Gospel According to Saint Luke. He asked the other Apostles what they knew about Jesus, and their stories are told in his Gospel. He travelled with Saint Paul all over the world. He told people that although he could heal their bodies, only Jesus could heal their souls. He painted a lovely picture of the Blessed Virgin. We still have copies of it. In the end, the pagans of Greece killed him because they hated Jesus. His Feast is October 18th.

St. Margaret—Mary

We all know how much God loves us. He created us out of nothing. He died for our sakes. He stayed with us in the Blessed Sacrament. But men and women forget God so quickly. He asks them to love Him. Instead they love all kinds of sinful and silly things. Once on a time, there was a very holy nun named Sister Margaret Mary. She loved Our Dear Lord with all her heart. She was sorry that everyone did not love Him too.

One day He appeared to her. He showed her His Sacred Heart. "Behold the Heart that has loved men so much," He said. And He asked her to tell others about His love for them. So Margaret Mary told everyone about the Sacred Heart. She loved Jesus Christ with all her heart herself. She brought millions to love Him too. She is the saint of Sacred Heart of Jesus. Her Feast is: October 17th.

Saint Martin—Bishop

The father and mother of Martin did not believe in God. So when Martin wanted to become a Christian, they wouldn't let him. Instead, his father put him into the army when he was only fifteen. Martin was a good soldier. Though most of the soldiers were not Christians, he loved Our Lord.

One winter night, Martin met a poor beggar, freezing in the snow. Martin had no money, so he took his sword, cut his cloak in half and gave one half to the beggar. That night, Our Lord came to him wearing the half cloak. He heard Jesus say to the angels, "Look, though Martin is not yet baptized, he gave Me his garment." So Martin became a Christian and converted his parents too. Because he was brave and strong, the people asked him to stop being a soldier and become their bishop. He did. He is one of the great apostles of France. His Feast is November 11th.

Saint Matthew—Writer of the Gospel

Once upon a time there was a tax gatherer named Levi. The Jews did not like him. He took their tax money and gave it to the Romans. But Levi was not a bad man. He only did what he thought was his duty. One day Jesus saw him. He saw good in him that others did not see. "Come and follow Me!" Jesus said quietly to the tax gatherer. Levi looked up in surprise. He had never seen such a wonderful Man before. Why, it would be the greatest honor to be one of His followers! Instantly he got up. He left his table with all the money on it. He went after our Lord. And Jesus made him one of His twelve Apostles. He changed his name to Matthew. He wrote the wonderful Gospel According to Saint Matthew. He saw all that Jesus did. He heard all that Jesus said. He walked with Him and grew to love Him more and more. To make sure that the world would never forget Jesus. Matthew wrote all this down in his beautiful Gospel. Gospel, you know, means Good News. He died a blessed martyr.

With Saint Mark, Saint Luke and Saint John, he is one of the Four Evangelists. His Feast is September 21st.

Saint Mary of Egypt—Who Had Been a Sinner

When she was a very little girl, Mary of Egypt was a great sinner. Almost everyone heard about her. For she was very beautiful. She led so many people into sin. She was very bad. One day a crowd of people took ship for Jerusalem.

The king had just found the Cross on which our Lord was hung. Mary went along because she thought it fun to travel. She did not care about the Cross. But when they came to Jerusalem, she went with the rest to the church. Inside was the Cross. She tried to enter. She could not. Some unseen force held her as if she were chained. Suddenly, she knew how wicked she was. She turned and saw a picture of Our Lady.

"Mary," she cried, "Mary Magdalen saw the Cross. Please let me stand beside that other sinful woman." And she walked into the church. She knew that her sins had nailed Jesus to that Cross. She fell on her knees and cried and cried, repenting of all her sins. Then she went out into the desert. For years she lived alone. She prayed. She did penance for her sin.

In the end, a holy man found her body on the sands. He buried the sinner who had become a saint. Her Feast is April 9th.

St. Martha—Sister of Mary Magdalen and Lazarus

Often our dear Lord was tired.

Often He grew weary when wicked men hated Him and tried to capture Him. He would then go for a visit to His friends.

His friends were Lazarus and Mary and Martha. They had a sweet and peaceful house in Bethany. When He came to this house, He was happy.

Lazarus talked to Him. Mary sat at His feet and listened and loved Him.

But Martha was a busy housekeeper. She prepared the meals for our dear Lord.

When Lazarus, their brother, died, she and Mary sent for Jesus. All they said was, "The man You love is sick."

Jesus came Himself. In a wonderful miracle, He raised Lazarus from the dead. He gave their brother back to his sisters, Mary and Martha.

Martha was present on Calvary when Jesus died.

She saw Him after He rose on Easter Sunday.

Later she and her brother and sister went to France. They told the French about Jesus. Many of the Frenchmen and women believed and became Christians. Her Feast is: July 29th.

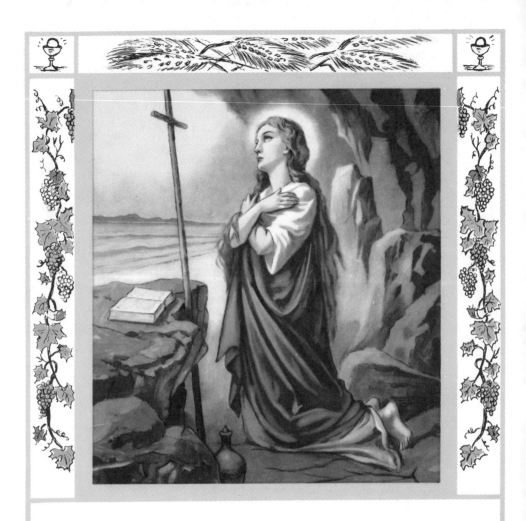

St. Mary—Magdalen

Once upon a time, Mary Magdalen was a great sinner. You see, she was very beautiful. So people paid her compliments. They ran after her and made her vain. She forgot that God gave her all her beauty. She loved rich clothes and fine jewels too much. She wanted to be popular at all costs. So she sinned. And she was very unhappy. Then one day, she saw Jesus, Our Lord. He looked at her and showed her how sorry He was about her sin. Right away, she knew how ugly sin was. She followed Jesus into the house of some rich men. Though they laughed at her, she knelt at His feet. She washed His feet with tears.

From that time on, she loved only Our Lord. She did not sin again. On Calvary, she stayed with Him until He died. After His resurrection, He showed Himself to her. Then, when He rose into Heaven, Mary Magdalen ran off into the desert. She wanted to spend all her time thinking of Him. Her Feast is: July 22nd.

St. Michael—Archangel

St. Michael is one of the Archangels. He is a warrior of God. Once upon a time long ago, the bad angels made war in Heaven. They cried, "We will not serve!" They raised the red flag. They tried to drive God from the Heavenly City. But Michael led the armies of the good angels. He drove out the evil army. He knelt before God and cried that God was his only King.

He is the Devil's strong enemy. He is the friend and protector of all those who love God and follow Jesus Christ. He is always on the side that is right and good. In the end of the world, a bad man named Antichrist will come. He will make war on Christ and the good people. But Michael and his army will drive him from the world. That is why we pray after Mass, "St. Michael, the Archangel, defend us in the day of battle." His Feast is: September 29th.

Saint Monica—Mother of Saint Augustine

Monica was a lovely young Roman girl. She was wonderfully pure and good. She loved Jesus very much. But her father loved money and power. So he made her marry a young Roman who was very rich. Monica worried about her dear husband. She prayed hard that he would become a Catholic. She set him a good example. And a year before he died, he asked to be baptized. But Augustine, her son, was her real worry. Like his father, he did not care for the Catholic faith, and he led a wild and wicked life. "I wish you would stop praying for me," he told her. But Monica prayed and prayed. "Don't worry," a holy priest told her, "your son cannot be lost, not after all your prayers and tears."

So Monica followed Augustine to Rome. To her joy, she found that he had completely changed his life. He was a Catholic. He had given up his sins and his evil companions. She thanked God. She died in peace knowing that her son was going to be a great saint and a great teacher and writer of Catholic truth. Her Feast is May 4th.

Saint Philip Neri—The Cheerful Saint

When Philip Neri was a young boy he lived in Rome. He had a terrible temper. He was afraid that some day he would flare up and hurt some one badly. So he set himself to cure his temper. He determined always to be cheerful. He learned to smile all the time. He loved to laugh. He was always pleasant. People loved just to see him and have him speak to them. Especially he loved the Holy Spirit. Indeed, once the Holy Spirit was seen to come down upon the young Philip. He shone with the light of the Third Person of the Trinity.

Philip became a priest. He started a little church in which he gathered friends. They prayed together. They sang together. He said Mass for them. They walked in happy processions through the streets. They crowned the statue of Our Lady. The little church was called the Oratory. That means, it was a lovely place to pray. People came to him sad. He sent them away happy. They came with their sins. He sent them away pure in soul. Children followed him. Sinners saw how lovely it is not to sin. He made evil men love God. He taught everyone the happiness of goodness. They called him the Apostle of Rome. His Feast is May 26th.

Saint Matilda

Matilda's father was a Saxon count. His name was Theodoric. Matilda's parents wanted her to be pious. They placed her in the Monastery of Exford.

There Matilda worked and prayed. She studied hard. She loved her work. She loved her parents. She loved her prayer and her spiritual reading. She became a model of virtue. Matilda's parents gave her in marriage. Her husband became the German King and Matilda the Queen.

She was a good queen. While her husband went to war and enlarged his kingdom, Matilda won victories over spiritual enemies. She knew this was more worthy of a Christian. She was a pious queen. She helped the sick. She taught ignorant people about Jesus and helped them become Catholics. She spent much time in prayer.

Matilda founded many churches and five monasteries. Her great pleasure was to teach the poor and ignorant how to pray. Matilda taught her people how to seek true virtue. "The beginning," she said, "is to want it and to ask it of God." Her feast is March 14.

St. Patrick—of Ireland

Patrick's name was a very noble one. It was taken from a Latin name that meant "a nobleman." Everyone loves Patrick, so many countries say he was born there. But wherever he was born, he became the friend of all and the Apostle of Ireland. The Irish in those days did not know about Jesus and Mary. Patrick felt very sorry for them. He studied hard, and became a priest and a bishop. The Pope sent him to Ireland to make it Catholic. The people of Ireland welcomed him with joy. The kings sat and listened to him.

He taught them about the Blessed Trinity by showing them how the Shamrock had three leaves yet was one plant. He drove all evils out of Ireland as if they were snakes. Soon he built churches and schools everywhere. Since St. Patrick's time, the Irish have carried the love of Jesus and Mary all over the world. That's why everyone loves St. Patrick and keeps his feast day. His Feast is: March 17th.

St. Paul—Apostle

At first his name was Saul. He hated Jesus Christ and all who believed in Him. He helped the men who killed St. Stephen, the first Martyr. Next he got an order from the judges to arrest Christians everywhere and put them to death. But as he rode away to do this, a light struck him from his horse. The voice of Jesus called him. Saul was deeply sorry. He believed in Jesus Christ. He became one of His greatest Apostles.

He travelled on land and sea to tell people about Our Lord. He taught the simple. He talked to the learned. He was shipwrecked. He was thrown into prison. But nothing stopped him from preaching Christ and His Cross. Thousands believed in Jesus because of this great man. God changed his name to Paul. He wrote beautiful letters called Epistles. In the end, he was killed with St. Peter in Rome. St. Peter and Paul are both buried in the great Church of St. Peter. His Feast is: June 30th.

St. Peter—Apostle

Simon was a fine fisherman when Jesus called him to be an Apostle. "I will make you a fisher of men," said Jesus. Later he became the Rock, for he was brave and strong. But often he boasted and ran into temptation. Our Lord made him his special friend. He explained everything important to him. One night, He even let Simon walk on the water.

Then one day, Simon made a great act of faith in Christ. Our Lord changed his name to Peter, which means The Rock. He made him the Head of His Church. Peter was the first pope. Yet when Our Lord was arrested, Peter was afraid. He told everyone he was not an Apostle. But when he wept bitterly, Jesus forgave him. He made him chief Shepherd of His flock. Peter ruled the Church bravely. In the end, he died, nailed to a cross, upside down. His Feast is: June 29th.

Saint Pius X—Pope

When he was a boy Joseph Sarto was called Bepi. He lived in Italy. His family were very poor. Bepi studied hard and when he grew up he became a priest. He loved God so much that he loved everyone just as God said we should.

He became a Bishop and when he was elected Pope he took the name Pius X. He did many wonderful things for children. He said that they should all be taught catechism so that they would know what the Church teaches. He said that they should make their First Communion as soon as they knew right from wrong and that they should receive Holy Communion often. Pius X's motto was "to restore all things in Christ" and that is what he spent his life trying to do.

His Feast is August 20th.

Saint Rita

When Rita was a little girl, she wanted to be a Sister. Instead, her Mother and Father made her marry a cruel, bad tempered husband. But though he was unkind to her, Rita was a good wife. She had twin boys whom she loved very much. But her husband had many enemies. One day, some of these men killed him. Her sons, now young men, were very angry. "We will kill the men who murdered our Father," they cried.

This is revenge and it is wrong.

Rita did not want them to commit mortal sin. She loved them. But she prayed to God to let them die rather than to commit a murder. Shortly after, God let them die. But first they confessed and received Holy Communion so that they went to Heaven.

Then Rita became an Augustinian nun. During her life and after her death, she worked many miracles. The Spaniards, because of her wonderful deeds, call her The Sweet Saint of the Impossible. Her Feast is May 22nd.

Saint Robert—The Monk

Robert was a young monk who lived in England. He heard that a group of holy young men wanted to love God very much. They wanted to be especially good to sinners. So he left his comfortable home and joined them. Soon other brave young men came. Together they built a beautiful monastery. There the poor could come for food. England had few hotels in those days. So travellers could stay over night in Robert's monastery. He gathered boys and girls to teach them about Jesus. He welcomed the sick and took care of them in his hospital. He never ate until the poor were fed. He gave away his own clothes. He sat up all night long to care for the sick. Once, as he was sitting at dinner, a friend gave him bread sweetened with honey. But through the window, he saw a poor man. He took the bread and honey, put it on a plate, and gave it to the poor man.

Next day, as he sat at dinner, the plate appeared in the air. It was bright and shining like gold. Then the monks knew that the poor man to whom Robert had given the bread and honey was Christ Himself. When Robert died, his soul, like a bright ball of fire, went straight up into heaven. The monks heard God's voice saying, "Enter into heaven!" His Feast is June 7th.

St. Rose—of Lima

This little girl is an American saint. She was born in Lima in Peru. Columbus had discovered America less than one hundred years before. Her name was really Isabel. But she was so beautiful that people called her Rose. Her parents were poor. So little Rose became a maid servant. Everybody noticed how beautiful she was. That made her afraid. Perhaps her good looks might lead her into sin. So she cut her lovely hair. She worked until her hands were rough. She wore old, unattractive clothes. She wanted her soul to be beautiful. Only God could see that. Then she decided to become a Dominican nun.

So many people around her were sinful. Rose wanted to do penance for their sins. She lived in a little hut. She slept on the floor. She begged God to forgive sinners. When the fleet of her country's enemies attacked Peru, her prayers drove them away and saved her city. When she died, all Peru wept. Her Feast is: August 30th.

Saint Rose—of Viterbo

Saint Rose was only eighteen when she died. But she was already a holy and a famous person. As soon as she could walk, she toddled straight to Jesus in the Tabernacle. As soon as she could talk, she talked about Jesus and heaven and God. There was a wicked king named Frederick in those days. He hated the Pope and made war on him. One day some of his friends came to her city. They made speeches against the Pope. They threatened to do wicked things to him. Little Rose was only ten years old.

Without fear, she rushed into the public square. She pushed the wicked men aside. She stood before the people of her city. "Do not listen to these men," she cried. "The Pope is the Vicar of Jesus Christ. Love him and protect him." The people were amazed at this little girl. But they followed her and were true to the Pope. When still a little girl, she became a nun. Then she went to a little convent in her city. She prayed. She cared for the poor.

She died, and her body after death remained beautiful and fragrant. Her Feast is September 4th.

Saint Sebastian—The Soldier

Sebastian was a captain in the Roman army, a fine officer and a brave soldier. One day he heard about Jesus Christ and said, "He is the one I want to follow." So from that day he loved Christ and fought bravely for Him. One day his two brothers were arrested. "You are Christians, and you must die," said the judge. They were only boys, and they were afraid. But Sebastian comforted them, saying, "Don't be afraid. We shall all be martyrs. It is glorious to die for Christ."

The Mayor of Rome did not believe in Jesus Christ. He heard about Sebastian and sent for the young soldier. "Tell me about Jesus," he ordered. And Sebastian talked so beautifully that the Mayor became a Christian too. This made the people who hated Jesus very angry. They began to kill the Christians. Many of the Christians fled from Rome. Although Sebastian helped them escape he refused to leave. So the Romans arrested Sebastian. They tied him to a stake. Soldiers shot at him with bows and arrows. They left him for dead. But Sebastian was not dead. He was still alive and he went to the judge who had ordered him shot. "Please believe in Jesus," he begged. But instead they beat him to death with clubs. His Feast is January 20th.

Saint Scholastica—The Benedictine

Saint Benedict was the first of the holy monks. Saint Scholastica was his beloved sister. He built monasteries for holy men. She built convents for holy women. Those were evil days and were full of dangers for good women. Bands of wicked soldiers roamed all over the world. So Saint Scholastica built lovely convents. They were full of peace. Women came there and were safe. Saint Benedict loved his sister very much.

One day, he sat and talked with her about God. Night came and he said, "I must go back to my home." "Please don't go," she said. For she knew she was going to die. When her brother, Benedict, insisted upon leaving, she bowed her head and prayed. Suddenly a great storm burst. The wind blew. The rain fell. The lightning flashed. Benedict could not go back. So all night long they sang together, they prayed together, they talked about God.

Three days later, Scholastica died. And Benedict saw her soul going up to heaven in the form of a pure, white dove. Her Feast is February 10th.

St. Stephen—the First Martyr

Stephen loved Jesus very much. He worked hard for the poor. He told everyone that Christ was their Savior. So many people followed him. They listened while he spoke. For his eyes were bright with love for Jesus. And he spoke beautifully of what Jesus had taught and done. One day the enemies of Jesus said, "We must stop this man. We killed Jesus. But this Stephen still makes others believe in Jesus. We must kill him too."

First they ordered him to stop preaching. He laughed. He could not stop talking about the Savior he loved. So they caught him. They dragged him outside the city. He told them that Jesus was not dead but had ascended into heaven. Angrily, they picked up rocks. They flung them at Stephen. He fell dead. But first he saw Jesus coming to take him. He was the first martyr. His Feast is: December 26th.

Saint Teresa—The Carmelite

There were two great Saint Teresas. One is called the Little Flower. The other is called the Great Saint Teresa. She was the Holy Mother of the Carmelite Sisters. The Little Flower was one of her lovely spiritual children. When the Great Teresa was a little girl, she ran away from home. Later she became a sister. She grieved for all the sinners in the world who did not love God "I will love Him all the harder because they do not," she said.

"Dear God," she prayed, "forgive them. See! I will suffer and do penance for their sins." So she slept on hard boards. She never ate meat. She prayed long hours. She said to God, "Please let me love You. Please let me suffer for their sins. And do not punish the people who hate You and who are wicked." Many holy young women joined her. They prayed for sinners. They asked God to keep young people from temptation. They loved God like dear daughters. And the Great Teresa built convents for them all over the world.

They are the Carmelite Nuns. Her Feast is October 15th.

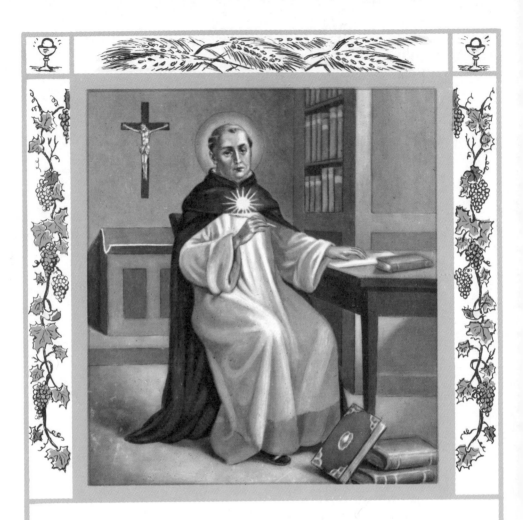

St. Thomas—Aquinas

Thomas Aquinas was a Dominican priest. His family did not want him to be a priest. They tried very hard to stop him. But he longed to say mass and preach. In the end, he won. Thomas became a great student. He learned to know all about Our Lord and His teachings. Young people came from all over the world to listen to his classes. He wrote a wonderful book called the Summa. Priests and wise men still study it today.

But he also wrote beautiful poetry and hymns. The hymns you sing at Benediction were written by Thomas. One day Our Lord, hanging on the cross, said to Thomas: "You have written well about Me, Thomas. What reward do you wish?" "Only yourself," answered the saint. He knew that if he had Jesus, he had everything. The Church calls him the Teacher who was like an Angel. His Feast is: March 7th.

St. Teresa—The Little Flower

This little saint lived in our times. She was a little French girl named Teresa Martin. Even as a little girl, she wanted to belong to God alone. Since people said, "You are too young," she asked the Pope to let her be a sister. So she entered the convent when still a child. She joined the Carmelites. She said, "I just want to love God. I want to do hard things for Him. I want to pray for priests and for sinners. I want to shine like a little candle before His altar."

Almost nobody knew about this little girl. But the minute she died, all the world seemed to hear about her. They read her story and loved her. Soldiers chose her as their patroness. She became the saint of French aviators. Priests asked her to take care of them. Catholic missions were helped with her prayers. Before she died, she said: "After death, I will drop down from Heaven a shower of roses." She did just that. Teresa, has filled the world with her miracles. Her Feast is: October 3rd.

Saint Ursula—and her Companions

When Ursula was a little girl, she loved children very much. She therefore became a teacher. Mothers and fathers sent their boys and girls to her. She taught them how to be good. She told them about Jesus and Mary. She had a fine school for them in England. But terrible pagan armies came into England. They threatened to kill all Christians. So Ursula took her pupils and her other teachers and went with them to France. But once again, she met peril.

The terrible Huns came with their armies. They hated Jesus Christ and they killed all Christians. So they captured Ursula and her sweet young companions. They asked Ursula to let them make slaves of the little boys and girls. Ursula refused. They promised to let them all go free if they would give up Christ and the Catholic faith. They all refused.

So the army of the Huns drew their swords. They pulled back their bows and arrows. They killed Ursula and all her companions. And like glorious martyrs they went straight to heaven. Her Feast is on October 21st.

St. Vincent—de Paul

Vincent de Paul was a very holy priest. He remembered how Our Lord loved the poor and worked for them. So he did all he could to make life sweet and easy for them. He gave them whatever money he had. He carried the poor sick home and took care of them in his own house. When he found poor children, he gave them food, clothing, toys, and his love. But always he told them about Jesus Christ. He told them that the Savior was poor too, and loved the poor most of all.

Once he was captured by pirates and carried away to sea. But he made the pirate himself love Jesus Christ and became a Catholic. To help him work for the poor, he gathered fine men and women about him. They continued his work after he died. The men are called Priests of the Mission. The women are the Sisters of Charity who do so much for the poor. His Feast is: July 19th.

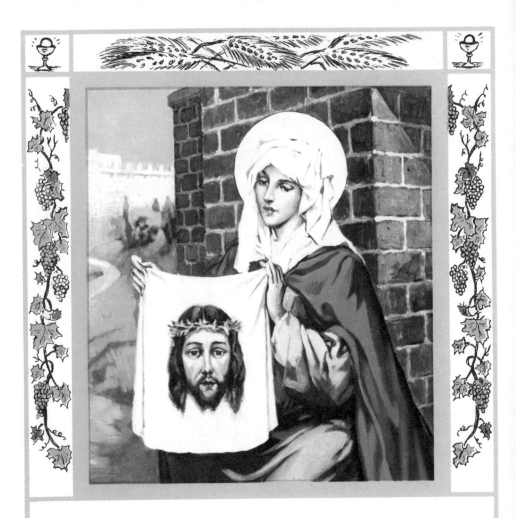

St. Veronica—of the Way of the Cross

We only know of one important incident in the life of Saint Veronica. This took place on the terrible day of our dear Lord's Passion. Jesus was carrying His cross. All around Him the people were laughing and screaming. They were throwing mud in His face. They were spitting upon Him. They tripped Him and made Him fall. Jesus looked around and saw no friends. Everyone seemed to hate Him. Then Veronica came. She wanted to help Him.

So she took the veil off her head. She pushed the soldiers aside. She ran through the crowd. She came to Jesus. He had just fallen and He was too weak to stand up. Lovingly she wiped His face with her veil. Jesus looked up gratefully. He thanked her with a smile. The soldiers pushed her away. But when she got home and looked at her veil, she found a wonderful thing. On the veil was a beautiful picture of Jesus. Her Feast is: July 9th.

Saint William—Archbishop

William was a rich young man. He was sent to fine schools. Everyone expected him to lead an exciting, successful life. Instead, he wanted to follow Our Lord very closely. If Jesus worked hard, he wanted to work hard too. If Jesus was poor, he preferred to be poor. Since Jesus was busy about His Father's business, young William wished this for himself. So he became a priest when he was very young. He studied hard. He prayed well. And when he preached, people loved to listen. But even this was not enough. He joined the poorest and hardest order of monks, called Cistercians.

He loved the prayer, peace, and quiet there. Yet the people wanted him back to care for them. So the Pope made him Archbishop of Bourges. He did not want the honor, but he obeyed the Holy Father. William never ate meat, though he gave it to his guests and the poor. He spent no money on himself, but all on the church, the school, and the needy.

When he died, all the people followed his body to the grave, weeping. His Feast is January 10th.

St. Francis Xavier—the Missionary

Saint Francis Xavier went to the University of Paris.

He was a champion runner. He was a great athlete.

In class, he was the leader. He studied hard.

"I want to be a great professor," he said. "I want to know all there is to know. I want people to listen when I talk. I want to write wonderful books."

Then he met Saint Ignatius Loyola. "What good will it do you," Ignatius asked him, "if you win the whole world and then lose your soul?"

Francis thought this over. He decided he could win the world and at the same time save his soul. So he became a friend of Saint Ignatius. He became a Jesuit. "Send me out," he said, "and I will win the world for our Lord."

So Ignatius sent him out as a missionary.

He went to India. He told people there about Jesus.

He went to Japan. The pagans listened. Many of them too became Catholics.

Then he wanted to go to China. Instead, he died on a little island just off the coast of China. But he had converted thousands and thousands.

He was the greatest missionary since the Apostles. His Feast is: Dec. 3rd.